Disaster!

The Titanic
The Tragedy at Sea

by Kathleen W. Deady

CAPSTONE
HIGH-INTEREST
BOOKS

an imprint of Capstone Press
Mankato, Minnesota

Capstone High-Interest Books are published by Capstone Press
151 Good Counsel Drive, P.O. Box 669, Mankato, Minnesota 56002
http://www.capstone-press.com

Library of Congress Cataloging-in-Publication Data
Deady, Kathleen W.
    The Titanic: the tragedy at sea/by Kathleen W. Deady.
    p. cm.—(Disaster!)
    Summary: Describes the giant ocean liner "Titanic," the events that led
up to its sinking in the spring of 1912, and the effects of the disaster on
sea travel.
    Includes bibliographical references and index.
    ISBN 0-7368-1323-3 (hardcover)
    1. Titanic (Steamship)—Juvenile literature. 2. Shipwrecks—North
Atlantic Ocean—Juvenile literature. [1. Titanic (Steamship) 2. Shipwrecks.]
I. Title. II. Disaster! (Capstone High-Interest Books)
G530.T6 D43 2003
910'.9163'4—dc21   2001008333

Editorial Credits
Matt Doeden, editor; Karen Risch, product planning editor; Kia Adams, designer;
    Jo Miller, photo researcher

Photo Credits
Bettmann/CORBIS, cover, 4, 6, 10 (left), 22, 25
Christie's Images/CORBIS, 10 (right)
CORBIS, 13
Hulton Archive by Getty Images, 12, 15, 16, 19
Mansell/Timepix, 20
Ralph White/CORBIS, 21, 27

**Special thanks to Dik Barton of RMS Titanic, Inc. for his help in preparing
this book.**

1 2   3   4   5   6   07   06   05   04   03   02

Table of Contents

Features

Fast Facts about the *Titanic*

Length: 882 feet, 9 inches
(269 meters)

Width: 92 feet (28 meters)

Height: 104 feet (32 meters)

Weight: 46,328 tons
(42,029 metric tons)

Cost to Build: $7.5 million

First Voyage: Began April 10, 1912

Date Sank: April 15, 1912

People Aboard: 2,228

Survivors: 705

CHAPTER ONE

The Disaster

On April 10, 1912, the giant ocean liner RMS *Titanic* floated in a harbor in Southampton, England. Crew members prepared *Titanic* for its first voyage as passengers boarded the ship.

Titanic was the largest ocean liner in the world. Some people said the ship was so large and sturdy that it was unsinkable. Newspapers around the world printed stories about the new ship.

Iceberg, Right Ahead!

At noon, *Titanic* Captain Edward J. Smith guided the ship slowly out of the harbor. Thousands of people gathered to watch the ship head out to sea. *Titanic* stopped in France and Ireland to pick up more passengers, then began the journey toward New York City.

An iceberg ripped several holes in the side of the *Titanic*'s hull.

On April 14, Seaman Frederick Fleet was posted in the crow's nest high above the main part of the ship. His job was to watch for danger ahead. About 20 minutes before midnight, he spotted a large, dark shape. Fleet shouted to officers aboard the ship's bridge, "Iceberg, right ahead!"

Officers on *Titanic*'s bridge quickly reversed the ship's engines and steered to the left. Slowly, the huge ship began to turn away from the iceberg, but it was too late. *Titanic* scraped against the edge of the iceberg. The iceberg ripped several holes in the side of the ship's hull.

Few of *Titanic*'s passengers noticed the crash, but Smith knew something was wrong. He hurried to the bridge from his cabin. At first, the crew thought the iceberg had done little damage. But they soon discovered that the lower decks of the ship were flooding.

By 11:50, water in the front of the ship was 14 feet (4.3 meters) deep. Smith realized the ship could not stay afloat. He also knew *Titanic* did not carry enough lifeboats for everyone aboard.

The Sinking

Smith ordered his officers to send a distress signal. He hoped another ship nearby would be able to come to *Titanic*'s rescue. Officers aboard the *Carpathia* received the signals from *Titanic*. The *Carpathia* was 58 miles (93 kilometers) away.

By 12:45, the first lifeboat was ready. Many people still did not understand the danger. Only 28 women and children sat in a lifeboat designed to carry 65 people.

Titanic's lower decks continued to flood. By 1:00, the front of the ship was sinking under the water's surface. People began to push their way into lifeboats. By 2:05, the last lifeboat was in the water. More than 1,500 people were still aboard the ship.

The rear of *Titanic* rose out of the water as the front end sank. Many people fell or jumped into the cold water below. The ship's lights flickered and went out. The huge ship then broke in two.

The front half of the ship disappeared beneath the water. The back slammed down against the surface and filled with water. At 2:20, the rear of the ship slid under the ocean surface.

Many people drowned as they were pulled underneath the water when *Titanic* sank. Some died as parts of the ship fell on them. Others froze in the icy water of the North Atlantic.

From a distance, survivors aboard lifeboats watched *Titanic* sink. Later, a few boats went back to look for more survivors. They found only four people still alive. One of these people died soon after being rescued.

The *Carpathia* arrived at about 4:10. Only 705 survivors remained.

The *Titanic*'s Voyage

ATLANTIC OCEAN

New York City

UNITED STATES

N
W   E
S

IRELAND
Queenstown

ENGLAND
Southampton
Cherbourg

FRANCE

Map Legend

Location of sinking

Planned Route

Learn About:

White Star Line

Building *Titanic*

Passenger classes

WHITE STAR LINE.

To NEW Yo
From SOUTHAMPTON-CHERBOURG-QUEENS
From LIVERPOOL-QUEENSTOWN.
To BOST
From LIVERPOOL-QUEENSTOWN.

For Freight and Passage apply to

THOS. COOK & SON,   31, Fargate, SHE
16, Clumber Street
97, Derby
and Gallowtree G.

"OLYMPIC."
45,000 TONS.
AND
"TITANIC."
45,000 TONS.
HE LARGEST STEAMERS
IN THE WORLD.

K.

TTINGHAM;
ESTER.

CHAPTER TWO

History and Design

In the early 1900s, ocean liners were the main transportation for people between Europe and North America. White Star Line was one company that operated ocean liners. In 1907, officials at White Star Line decided to build the biggest ocean liner in history.

J. Bruce Ismay was managing director for White Star Line. He met with a shipbuilder named Lord William James Pirrie to make plans to build several huge ocean liners. The largest of these ships would be called *Titanic*.

Building *Titanic*

Workers began building *Titanic* in 1909. They had never before built such a large ship. *Titanic* was 882 feet, 9 inches (269 meters) long and 92 feet (28 meters) wide. It had nine decks and stood 104 feet (32 meters) tall. *Titanic* weighed 46,328 tons (42,029 metric tons).

Twenty-nine boilers produced *Titanic*'s power. Each boiler weighed about 100 tons (91 metric tons). These boilers burned coal to boil water and produce steam. The steam powered the ship's engines.

Titanic's engines powered three huge propellers. The propellers turned in the water to push *Titanic* forward or backward. One propeller was 16 feet (4.9 meters) wide. The other two were more than 23 feet (7 meters) wide.

Titanic's huge propellers pushed the ship through the water.

Ship Design

People called the *Titanic* a floating palace. It had restaurants, a gym, and four elevators. *Titanic* was the first ship with a swimming pool. It even had courts for a racket game called squash.

Titanic was designed to carry a variety of passenger classes. Most of the ship's space was for first-class passengers. These passengers stayed in large cabins. They were free to go anywhere on the ship. First-class passengers each paid about $4,350 for the trip.

Second-class passengers paid about $65 for the trip. They stayed in small rooms near the rear of the ship. They were not allowed to go to some areas of *Titanic* reserved for first-class passengers.

Third-class passengers stayed in small rooms on the lower decks. They were not allowed on the upper decks. They paid about $35 for the trip.

Titanic was designed for safety. The lower hull had 16 separate compartments. The designers said these divided sections were airtight. The ship could still float even if four compartments filled with water. Many people believed this feature made *Titanic* unsinkable.

Some people called *Titanic* a floating palace because it had so many rooms.

Learn About:

Government inquiries

Ignored warnings

Lifeboat shortage

CHAPTER THREE

What Went Wrong

Shortly after the sinking, the governments of both the United States and England held official inquiries about the disaster. They questioned many people who survived the sinking. They tried to understand how such a large ocean liner could sink. They also tried to find ways to prevent such a disaster from happening again.

Iceberg Warnings

Inquiry officials learned that the *Titanic* crew had received iceberg warnings before the accident. They wondered why *Titanic* had not slowed down. The ship might have avoided the iceberg if it had been traveling at a slower speed.

Officials also wondered why the *Titanic* crew had not seen the iceberg sooner. Crew members aboard ocean liners usually use binoculars to search for dangerous objects ahead. *Titanic's* crew had not been using binoculars. The ship was already too close to the iceberg when the crew spotted it.

Inquiry officials could not easily learn the answers to these questions. Captain Smith had died in the accident. Second Officer Charles Lightoller was the highest ranking survivor. But he did not know the answers to many of the questions. Inquiry officials could only guess why *Titanic's* crew did not see the iceberg.

Titanic's captain, Edward J. Smith, died in
the disaster.

Lifeboat Shortage

Officials also wondered why *Titanic* carried so few lifeboats. Only 16 full-sized boats and four smaller boats were aboard *Titanic*. These boats could hold only 1,178 people when they were fully loaded.

Some officials accused White Star Line of using poor judgment by not including

Titanic carried its lifeboats on the edges of the upper decks.

enough lifeboats. These officials said White Star Line had included so few lifeboats because the boats took space on the deck. Much of *Titanic*'s deck space was for first-class passengers.

White Star Line officials said that *Titanic* carried more lifeboats than the law required. But the lifeboat laws were old. The number of lifeboats required depended on the weight of the ship. The laws did not account for huge ocean liners carrying thousands of people.

Another part of the problem was that *Titanic*'s crew had never held lifeboat drills. Crew and passengers were not sure how to load lifeboats quickly. Many of the first lifeboats went out with fewer people than they were supposed to carry.

Titanic's lifeboats could carry only 1,178 people when fully loaded. This number was only enough to carry about half of the people aboard the ship.

Learn About:

International Ice Patrol

New laws

Finding *Titanic*

CHAPTER FOUR

What We Have Learned

The sinking of *Titanic* showed people around the world the dangers of icebergs in the North Atlantic. After the accident, the U.S. government worked with the governments of many European countries to form the International Ice Patrol. This organization tracks icebergs throughout the North Atlantic and warns ships about icebergs in the area. Not one ship has been lost because of an iceberg collision since the patrol began.

New Safety Rules

Many people died in the *Titanic* disaster because laws for ocean liners were outdated. The laws were put in place before ships as large as *Titanic* had been built. Governments quickly passed new laws to solve some of the problems *Titanic* had faced.

Lifeboat laws were among the most important new laws. Ships were required to have enough lifeboats to carry every person on board. Crew members and passengers were required to hold lifeboat drills before every voyage. Government officials hoped these laws would prevent confusion aboard ships in future disasters.

Communication laws also changed after the disaster. Each ship had to have at least one officer listening for signals from other ships at all times. A special radio frequency was set aside just for distress signals from ships in trouble.

The *Titanic* disaster caused many countries to pass laws requiring ocean liners to carry more lifeboats.

25

Lost and Found

Some people wanted to find *Titanic* after it sank. But no one knew exactly where the ship had gone down. The waters of the North Atlantic are very deep. At the time, people had no way to search so far underwater.

In 1985, Dr. Robert Ballard formed a team of explorers to search for *Titanic*. They studied maps and tried to guess where the accident may have occurred. The team then used a small unmanned submarine called *Argo* to search the ocean floor. A video camera aboard *Argo* showed Ballard and his team the ocean floor.

The team searched all over the North Atlantic. Finally, on September 1, *Argo* found *Titanic* 12,469 feet (3,800 meters) below the ocean surface. Scientists and explorers finally knew where the ship had sunk. The pictures *Argo* sent back showed that the two main pieces of the ship had fallen about 1,970 feet (600 meters) apart. Search teams were later able to bring some small items from *Titanic* back to the surface.

The story of *Titanic* still interests people today. Authors, artists, and photographers have published hundreds of books about *Titanic*. In 1997, Paramount Pictures released a movie about the disaster. It was one of the most popular movies of the year. The movie's success showed that people today remain interested in the sinking of the giant ocean liner.

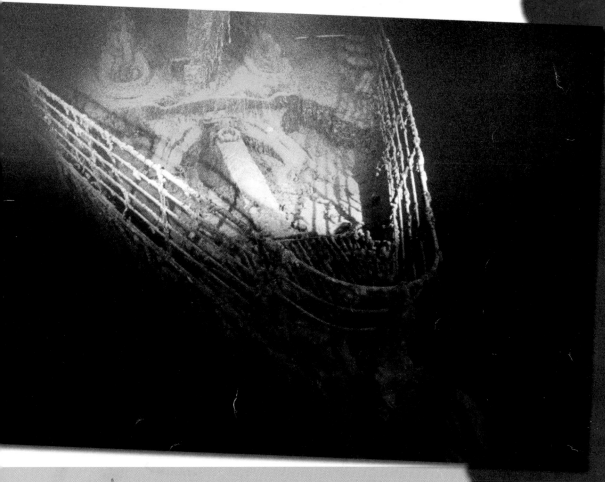

Today, *Titanic* rests 12,469 feet (3,800 meters) beneath the ocean surface.

Timeline

J. Bruce Ismay and Lord William James Pirrie discuss early plans for *Titanic*.

Workers begin building *Titanic*; at the time, it is the largest passenger ship ever built.

1907   **1908**   **1909**   **1911**

Ismay and Pirrie discuss the final plans for *Titanic*.

White Star Line launches *Titanic*.

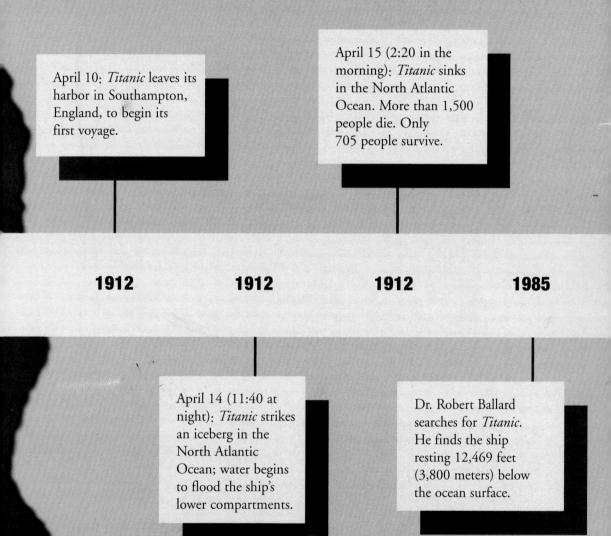

April 10: *Titanic* leaves its harbor in Southampton, England, to begin its first voyage.

April 15 (2:20 in the morning): *Titanic* sinks in the North Atlantic Ocean. More than 1,500 people die. Only 705 people survive.

1912   **1912**   **1912**   **1985**

April 14 (11:40 at night): *Titanic* strikes an iceberg in the North Atlantic Ocean; water begins to flood the ship's lower compartments.

Dr. Robert Ballard searches for *Titanic*. He finds the ship resting 12,469 feet (3,800 meters) below the ocean surface.

Words to Know

boiler (BOI-lur)—a tank that boils water to produce steam

bridge (BRIJ)—the control center of a ship; crew members aboard *Titanic* steered the ship from this room.

crow's nest (KROHZ NEST)—a lookout post located high above a ship

distress signal (diss-TRESS SIG-nuhl)—a call for help; officers aboard *Titanic* sent out a distress signal when the ship began to sink.

inquiry (IN-kwuh-ree)—an official investigation

propeller (pruh-PEL-ur)—a set of rotating blades that provides force to move a ship through water

To Learn More

Cole, Michael D. *The Titanic: Disaster at Sea.* American Disasters. Berkeley Heights, N.J.: Enslow, 2001.

Harmon, Daniel E. *The Titanic.* Great Disasters, Reforms, and Ramifications. Philadelphia: Chelsea House, 2001.

Jenner, Caryn. *Titanic: A Survivor's Tale.* Dorling Kindersley Readers. New York: Dorling Kindersley, 2001.

Useful Addresses

RMS Titanic, Inc.
3340 Peachtree Road NE
Suite 1225
Atlanta, GA 30326

Titanic Historical Society
P.O. Box 51053
208 Main Street
Indian Orchard, MA 01151-0053

Internet Sites

Titanic.com
http://www.titanic.com

Titanic: The Official Archive
http://www.titanic-online.com/titanic/index.html

A Tribute to the R.M.S. Titanic
http://www.fireflyproductions.com/titanic

Index